this HOLY ALPHABET

Lyric Poems
Adapted from
Psalm 119

D1521161

To Gloria,
with gratitude

MARGARET B. INGRAHAM

Margaret B Ingraham

this
HOLY
ALPHABET

Lyric Poems
Adapted from
Psalm 119

Foreword by
Rabbi Micah Greenstein

Preface by
Phyllis Tickle

PARACLETE PRESS
BREWSTER, MASSACHUSETTS

This Holy Alphabet: Lyric Poems Adapted from Psalm 119

2009 First Printing

Copyright © 2009 by Margaret B. Ingraham

ISBN: 978-1-55725-655-3

Library of Congress Cataloging-in-Publication Data

Ingraham, Margaret B.

 This holy alphabet : lyric poems adapted from Psalm 119 / Margaret B.

Ingraham ; foreword by Rabbi Micah Greenstein ; preface by Phyllis Tickle.

    p. cm.

 Includes bibliographical references and index.

 ISBN 978-1-55725-655-3

 1. Bible. O.T. Psalms CXIX--Paraphrases, English. I. Title.

BS1450119th I54 2009

223'.205208--dc22   2009038209

10 9 8 7 6 5 4 3 2 1

Published by Paraclete Press

Brewster, Massachusetts

www.paracletepress.com

Printed in the United States of America

For Meg and Chase

Table of Contents

Foreword

The power of this "holy Hebrew alphabet"
is hard to fully appreciate in English. In the ninth-century
Jewish text known as *Sefer Yetzirah*, "The Book of Creation," which
focuses on the origin of the universe, it is written, "With [the]
twenty-two letters [of the Hebrew alphabet], God engraved,
carved out, weighed, changed, combined and formed out of
them all existing forms in the universe, and all forms that may in
the future be called into existence." In other words, God created
the world by means of the twenty-two Hebrew letters.

Just as it is nearly impossible to grasp all the nuances
of Albert Camus' French writings or Verdi's Italian lyrics in
English, the same may be said in reading the Hebrew Bible in
general, and Psalms in particular. Rather than focusing on the
inner working of the letters, Margaret B. Ingraham renders
Psalm 119 in a new idiom by letting the themes of the verses
do their own talking.

Psalm 119, along with psalms such as 25, 34, and 111, is an acrostic in which each verse or section begins with a successive letter of the Hebrew alphabet. In Jewish tradition, it is customary to read a specific selection from this and other psalms when a person is gravely ill. In one of the magical applications of Psalm 119, verses are selected that spell out the letters of the name of the ill person, together with verses that start with the letters of the expression "Kera Satan" (root out Satan).

Psalm 119 is also used at life's supremely special moments. For instance, when a child enters the covenant of the Jewish people and is given his or her Hebrew name, it is customary to create an acrostic using the letters of the child's name and the matching alphabetical verses of the psalm itself.

Larger themes also emerge from this holy alphabet—including the repeated teaching of Torah as an eternal expression of God's love for us. The Torah is viewed as a vehicle by which we can find our way to this loving God (see verses 97, 113, 127, 163).

Perhaps what is most distinctive about the Psalms is that instead of God talking to the people, the Psalms comprise the only book of the Hebrew Bible wherein the people cry out to God. We hear that not only in times of joy and love, but in enduring suffering (v. 71) and in viewing our misfortunes as teachable moments (v. 67).

I applaud Margaret B. Ingraham's adaptation of Psalm 119 and hope it inspires all readers to probe the deeper meaning and mystery of the twenty-two holy letters with which God created the world.

—Rabbi Micah D. Greenstein

Preface

With the very simple act of opening this book, you and I have already begun to engage one of the world's most often used and devoutly reverenced pieces of sacred literature. That fact alone calls for far more of a preface than could ever be written by any human hand, while at the same time it makes any prefatory remarks at all seem superfluous, if not downright suspect. Together, those two statements constitute a brace of facts that I assure you I am very aware of at this particular moment.

The Hebrew Psalter is known to every Christian just as surely as it is to every Jew, albeit in differing, or at least variant, applications and circumstances. The same is true as well for adherents of the other of the Abrahamic faiths; for the Prophet taught that the Psalms were revealed to David in the way that Torah was revealed to Moses and must, therefore, be eternally honored and revered.

For its part, the Church catholic has, from its very beginning, employed the Psalms in all forms of corporate worship and, most particularly, in the keeping of the daily offices or hours of prayer. Calvin likewise taught the Reformation Church that the Psalter was the only acceptable hymn book; and in essence, Anglicanism fashioned its integral and unsurpassed *Book of Common Prayer* around it. Of the whole of the Psalter, however, no single poem/hymn is so treasured or so often employed as is Psalm 119.

As Rabbi Greenstein makes clear in his superb Foreword to this volume, Judaism by tradition has always turned to the 119th for ritualistic, as well as devotional, uses. Christianity has done so as well, turning to 119 for not only worship but also the study of the nuances of theology. At the time of his martyrdom, for example, Dietrich Bonhoeffer was working on, and left behind as unfinished, a study of Christian ethics based on his exegesis of 119. And Christians and Jews alike have always agreed in regarding the 119th as the most individualistic or personal of the Psalter's poem/hymns. For both faiths, it is, in its entirety, the record of a love affair with God ... a personal, as well as an aggregate, love affair.

Doctrinally—and especially for Christians and most especially for Protestant Christians—the 119th has also been the piece of Hebrew scripture that dealt most ferociously and grandly and intimately with the Word of God. The one hundred and seventy-six verses that compose Psalm 119 make it the longest psalm in the Psalter, but over and over again, those hundred and seventy-six dance with, praise, embrace, celebrate the Word as the law of God, the ordinances of God, the decrees of God, the path of God, the testimonies and precepts of God, the judgments of God, the statutes of God. Together, all those human words for the Word became a litany that rang, and still rings, with clarity and elegance in Christian ears.

Psalm 119 is an acrostic poem. That is, it is composed of twenty-two sections, each one of which commences with a letter, in sequence, of the Hebrew alphabet. There are nine such poems—such acrostic hymns—in the Psalter. By the very intricacy of their construction, those nine inevitably rivet the attention and command the respect of those of us, Christian or Jew or Muslim, who sink ourselves, our souls, and our spirits into their art. None of the nine, however, gives itself over with such perfection of phrase and image as does Psalm 119. Poetry's hold on our human imagination has long fascinated philosophers and wisdom teachers alike; for poetry is that singular form of art in which the tool of verbal thought is inextricably entwined with the corpus of nonverbal thought that is conveyed only in music. All too often, as most of us so painfully know, when poetry—even imagistically rich and finely honed poetry—is translated out of the language of its composition and into some other tongue, its music dies or, at best, becomes only a suggestion of its true or original self. Because of the stature of Psalm 119, the loss of its poetry in English translation has been most especially felt and regretted over the years.

There is no way to lift a suite of poetry from Hebrew to English and have equivalency of music. Margaret B. Ingraham seems to know that as completely and experientially as does any poet working in English today. But years of living with, and being tutored by, Psalm 119 in its Hebrew original also seem to have taught her how to achieve, if not an equivalency of exactitude, then at least an equivalency of similitude or effect. Using the tools of English poetry that are her stock in trade, she has created a Psalm 119 that is identical to its Hebrew forebear in thrust, fervor, and images; but she has mounted those things in a setting of English poetry. The result sometimes is stunning:

> Pull from Your pouch of justice
> The lot of grace for me,
> Mercy as right judgment
> For my iniquity.

Sometimes the underlying concepts are so familiar that Ingraham's gift is that of giving them back to us washed clean of their very familiarity:

> In Your word is my delight;
> Hidden within my heart as treasures.
> All Your promises bring me light ...

Sometimes the wording itself is wrenching enough so even the artifice of translation disappears into visceral experience:

> Once my soul had dropped from grief,
> You, O Lord, revived me.

Whatever the result may be within the individual souls, spirits, and devotion of each of us who enters here, however, one certain and more public result will be that of gratitude. As contemporary, English-speaking Christians, we have been blessed by the coming of this book, and any one of us who ponders here for a while will know it.

—Phyllis Tickle

Introduction

This is a small book that contains only twenty-two poems, or perhaps just a single poem of twenty-two sections. It can be read as either or as both. Like the text from which it is taken, it is designed to speak for itself. My hope is that it will. That said, providing some sense of context may be helpful.

This volume is a cycle of lyric poems that are *adaptations*, not translations, of Psalm 119. I am not sure how to explain the distinction between those two things precisely but I know that it is a significant one. If readers are expecting a new translation of a familiar work, they will not find it here. These poems are not translations but are based on translations—my own original translations from the Hebrew text of the *Biblia Hebraica Stuttgartensia* (BHS), which is regarded by both Jewish and Christian scholars as the definitive edition of the Hebrew Bible based on the masoretic texts.

I originally turned to that text for clarification when I found a verse of the psalm in a popular English translation perplexing. In other words, I did not approach the psalm with a well devised plan to write this book but as a part of my daily devotion and study. As I worked through the Hebrew, the masterful poetry of the psalm engaged me in a manner I have not experienced before, and it opened up my vision to conceive the project that became *This Holy Alphabet*.

Throughout the centuries poets writing in English have been drawn, as I was, to the psalms, and translations—fine translations in the ever-changing styles and vernaculars of our language over the decades—abound. To my knowledge, adaptations like this one are less common and no other has yet appeared in this new century.

Once I had envisioned the project, the method of completing it was clear. Only in going back to that original text, I believed, could I understand the subtleties of the Hebrew language and the imagistic and lyrical and rhetorical richness and complexities of this magnificent poem.

That is a fact that deserves reiteration. While I am unequivocal in my personal belief that the BHS is "Holy Writ in the Holy Tongue," as my Hebrew instructor was fond of reminding his students, the psalms are great literature as well— arguably the finest poetry ever written in any language, in any century, in any culture, and in any faith or secular tradition.

While Psalm 119 is clearly part of the same tradition as the other 149 poems in the Psalter, and while it shares a poetic voice with numerous ones of them—particularly those known to have been written by or attributed or dedicated to King David—this particular psalm stands out from all the others for a number of reasons. It is the longest of all the psalms and, in fact, is the longest chapter in both the Hebrew and Christian Bible.

Psalm 119 is also one of a small group of intricate acrostic poems from the book of Psalms. Within that group, it is the most elaborate and complex of them all. My purpose here is not to give a scholarly explanation of those complexities—or what C.S. Lewis more appropriately termed the "embroidery" of the poem. But one can understand neither the intention of the author who brilliantly and painstakingly wrote the psalm, nor its significance to Jewish worship and instruction throughout the millennia, nor even the heart of this small book, without some awareness of its form.

Like every acrostic psalm, this one relies on the twenty-two letters (consonants) of the Hebrew alphabet to give it structure. Each of the twenty-two sections of Psalm 119 begins with the successive consonant of the alphabet. So, the first letter of the first word of the first section is *aleph*, the equivalent of the English letter *a*; the second is *bet*, *b*; and so on. That kind of writing requires considerable rigor, as I found out while first attempting to preserve a portion of the acrostic nature of the poems as I adapted them.

But Psalm 119 also goes well beyond this simple acrostic pattern in its intricacy. In fact, in this psalm the first letter of the first word of every line (or, what in Hebrew poetry would be called a *stich*) in each section begins with the same letter. That is, the *aleph* section has eight lines, and each one of those lines begins with *aleph*. The same is true for the *bet* section, and the pattern is repeated through to the end of the psalm, the 176th *stich*.

In addition, all but two of the 176 *stiches*, which English has generally transformed into verses by breaking the line somewhere near the middle, contain one of nine Hebrew words. These words are translated as follows: *law* (*Torah*/ *teaching*/*instruction*); *testimony; way; precept; statute; commandment; judgment; saying*/*promise;* and *word*.

Throughout generations, for Jews and Christians alike, Psalm 119 has been regarded as a sort of instruction manual, containing all that one needed to know to live a holy and righteous life. Commentaries abound, from century after century until the present day, and their number and variety give testimony to the fact that those who have taken the time to study and meditate on Psalm 119 have found wisdom and blessing in it.

For some, however, the psalm's tightly structured pattern apparently seems more like an artifice than the psalmist's honest attempt to faithfully reflect what he sees of the orderliness and the fine and intricate design of what the Maker has done. The purpose of the repetition of words as more than simply a poetic device, but as both an effective method of instruction and a means of adoration and praise seems to have been lost on some modern readers. Many find it tedious; others suppose the psalmist is simply saying the same thing over and over again. Or they assume that, except for the need to complete the puzzle, some of the repetitions could easily be eliminated. I do not hold that view, although I certainly understand it. Part of my purpose here is to dispel those notions, not by argument or scholarship (neither of which I am qualified to claim or present), but by leading readers into the core of each section and letting the text itself, newly arranged and freshly stated, do its own talking.

That is why—or one of the principal reasons why— adaptation rather than strict translation was the approach I selected. The other reason was a far more practical one. I simply could not maintain even a limited acrostic pattern without rearranging or reordering some of the *stiches* or "verses" of each section. Sometimes the transition from Hebrew to English letter was easy, and the line sequences could be easily maintained. Other times it was more difficult, and in some cases required an invention on my part. *Tsade*, for example, for which there is no English counterpart, became z, the closest that I could come to single letter replication and remain faithful to the text.

While all of the poems in *This Holy Alphabet* rely on that kind of reordering and invention, let me stress that in every case I strove fastidiously to maintain the integrity of the text. That is why my process began first with transliteration from the Hebrew, then translation, and after that, adaptation. A good deal of my adaptation is technical and structural in nature and stems largely from the fact that ancient Hebrew poetry and modern English poetry have distinctly different characteristics and do not use the same forms. Hebrew poetry, for example, does not utilize rhyme or meter in the same sense that we who are accustomed to modern English verse understand. But most Hebrew poetry is inherently lyrical and achieves what is *like rhyme* by virtue of the fact that the Hebrew language has particular word endings (suffixes) that are repeated throughout. And it has music, if not a meter. It does not, however, utilize verses, per se.

What Hebrew poetry does share with English, and indeed all poetry in every tongue, is rich imagery and allusion. As I worked through these poems, I mined those images and references and attempted to present them in a fresh, though accurate, way—in a way that I hoped would engage a contemporary reader and open these ancient words and mysteries anew.

As much as the psalms are poems and prayers, they are also songs. Even today we find them in the synagogue and in liturgical Christian churches sung aloud or chanted as anthems or canticles, either by choirs and congregations or a single cantor. To demonstrate how this tradition might be practiced with these poetic sections, I have essentially set two of them to music by conforming them to a metrical pattern that fits familiar tunes found in various Christian hymnals. And I have referenced these tunes in the notes to the text.

Other sections may lend themselves to song and chant as well; in fact, by creating refrains I have structured some of the poems with the hope that they may find tunes in the future.

That said, it is not my place or my purpose to suggest to readers how this volume or its contents can best be used. But it is my desire that whenever and wherever and however it is read, it will evoke anew a sense of wonder and awe, in the power of language as building blocks not only of creation but also of praise, and of the holiness of God's alphabet, which to this day God uses to speak afresh to Jew and Christian alike.

Hallelujah!

Acknowledgments

This book would never have been conceived if my parents had not raised me in the Christian faith, and specifically in a liturgical church, where the psalms were a regular component of corporate worship as well as of private devotion, and if my Jewish friends had not invited me at an early age into their houses of worship. There I experienced firsthand Jewish liturgical traditions—the reading of Torah in Hebrew and the cantors' songs—and there I began to understand in a personal way what "Judeo-Christian" meant and to discover the profound connection of that faith tradition to my own. It is impossible to recognize every individual or institution that contributed to this project. So I can simply express my gratitude to the many whose lives have surrounded and sustained mine and hope that they will accept my heartfelt thanks.

There are some, however, whose roles have been particularly significant. First is Phyllis Tickle, whose contribution reaches far beyond her Preface. I have been blessed to have Phyllis as a mentor, teacher, friend, editor, collaborator, and encourager for more than three decades. Without her support over the years, there would be no *This Holy Alphabet*. I am also extraordinarily grateful to Paraclete Press for undertaking the publication of this work and specifically to Jon Sweeney for both his expert editorial guidance and his patience. My special thanks are due to Rabbi Micah Greenstein, who brings the gift of the Jewish perspective and a personal understanding of the great Hebrew wisdom literature to this volume. The Reverend Dr. William A. Weiler's love for the Holy Tongue and fine pedagogic skills opened the wonders of Hebrew to me. I am indebted to him, to the Virginia Theological Seminary for making his teaching and its facilities available to the laity, and to my fellow students for their mutual encouragement and perseverance in the study of a difficult language. Finally, I want to express my appreciation to the Virginia Center for the Creative Arts for providing the creative sanctuary where this book could come into being.

this
HOLY
ALPHABET

Psalm
119:1-8  ALEPH

Ah, happiness! Ah, truly blessed
are those who walk
inside the law of God.

Lord, may my heart be firm
to guard my every word,
to turn my eyes from wrong.
Do not forsake me.

Ah, happiness! Ah, truly blessed
are those who hold
Your precepts in their hearts.

Lord, may my soul be strong
to turn at Your command,
be guided by Your hand.
Do not forsake me.

אַשְׁרֵי תְמִימֵי

Ah, happiness! Ah, truly blessed
are those who walk
inside the law of God.

Lord, may my voice be free
to cast my praise on Thee,
to toss my shame away.
Do not forsake me.

Ah, happiness! Ah, truly blessed
are those who hold
Your precepts in their hearts.

Lord, may my heart be firm,
and may my soul be strong,
and may my voice be free.
Do not forsake me.

Ah, happiness! Ah, truly blessed
are those You hold
upright in righteousness.

אתיאה

Psalm
119:9-16 ב BET

(may be sung to the tune of Grosser Gott[1])

Blessed are You, O Lord of all;

With my heart I have sought to see You.

Blessed am I when I heed Your call,

Walk unswervingly by Your leading—

Follow on the path before

Which You lead me evermore.

I declare Your holy way;

Raise my voice to sing Your glory.

Ponder Your statutes night and day,

To claim the riches You stored up for me—

Follow on the path before

Which You lead me evermore.

---

[1] Melody from Katholisches Gesangbuch 1686, alt. Cantate, 1851.
Harmony, Charles Winfred Douglas (1867–1944), after Conrad Kocher (1786–1872).

In Your word is my delight;
Hidden within my heart as treasures.
All Your promises bring me light,
Keep me from vain sin and sorrow—
Follow on the path before
Which You lead me evermore.

עוֹלָה

ג GIMEL

Graciously, graciously
Deal with me graciously
Open my eyes to see
Surpassing wonders of Your word.

Long have I wandered off
Long has my soul been crushed
I am a stranger in the earth.

Graciously, graciously
Roll reproach far from me
Show me humility
Guarding Your law within my heart.

Long have I wandered off
Long has my soul been crushed
I am a stranger in the earth.

Gratefully, gratefully
Broken I come to Thee
Fall down on bended knee
Musing upon Your righteousness.

Long had I wandered off
Long had my soul been crushed
I was a stranger in the earth.

Graciously, graciously
With grace You dealt with me
Grateful I'll always be
Delighting in Your marvelous ways.

בְּעֵדוֹתֶיךָ
תְּבִישֵׁנִי :

Psalm
119:25-32 ד DALET

Dust of grief enshrouds my soul;
Now, O Lord, revive me.

All my wandering ways I've told;
Now, O Lord, revive me.

Cause me to discern Your ways,
Turn from falsehood and sing praise
Of Your marvelous works.

Once my soul had dropped from grief;
You, O Lord, revived me.

By Your word, You raised me up;
You, O Lord, revived me.

So enlarge my heart this day.
I will choose the faithful way.
Show me Your favor.

אֲשֶׁר יָגַרְתִּי

Psalm
119:33-40 **ה** HEY

(may be sung to the tune of Tallis' Canon)

Help me, O Lord, Your law to see
that I may keep it endlessly.
Make me discern Your holy way;
preserve it in my heart today.

Cause me to walk by Your command,
along the path to take Your hand.
And turn my heart from unjust gain
and turn my eyes from all that's vain.

Give life to me in Your just way
and raise Your servant up today.
Utter Your word so I may hear.
Pass over the reproach I fear.

Behold, I long for what is good.
I long to follow as I should.
Revive my heart to set it right.
Show me, O Lord, my soul's delight.

כָּל-מִצְוֹתֶיךָ

Psalm
119:41-48 **ו** VAV

Valiantly, Lord, I speak Your word,
give testimony to the world.
As I do, I'm not ashamed
because I trust what You have told.

You make me walk in a broad place
because I choose to keep Your law.
And bless me as I meditate
upon Your ways in humble awe.

Deliverance You give to me
by Your kindness mercifully.
Your lovingkindness meets me, Lord.
Salvation is Your gift to me.

Refrain:
I'll take delight in Your commandments,
which I have loved;
I'll raise my palms at Your commandments,
which I have loved.

Repeat Refrain.

עַד-מֵאֹז
נָטִיתִי.

Psalm
119:49-56 ז ZAYIN

Zeal has overtaken me and my songs of praise flow forth
as I remember all that You have done.

Out of my poverty, Your quickening words have lifted me
and I have taken comfort in Your hope.

The proud have scorned me utterly while they forsake
Your law but I journey on holding fast Your truth.

Your eternal judgments, I have learned well, will ever stand
and in that way my heart has been consoled.

Recalling Your holy name, O Lord, as the evening comes
has drawn me with comfort into Your keep.

Speak Your word to me in my house of earthly sojourning
so I may remain faithful all my days.

אֶל-עֵדֹתֶיךָ

Psalm
119:57-64

ח CHET

Cords of guilt coiled round about me
Cannot keep me from Your ways.
Though these cords of guilt surround me
Yet I rise to sing Your praise.

You, Lord, are my territory,
You, the land my heart calls home.
You, the one who shows me favor,
You are my righteous judge alone.

Cords of guilt coiled round about me
Will not keep me from Your ways.
When these cords of guilt surround me
Still I rise to sing Your praise.

I have made Your holy face sweet
Turning my feet toward Your commands;
You made me a true companion
To all who are Your faithful band.

Cords of guilt coiled round about me
Do not keep me from Your ways.
When these cords of guilt surround me
Then I rise to sing Your praise.

I have seen, O Lord, Your kindness
Spread throughout the earth this day.
Teach me, teach me, Lord, Your statutes
So I may hasten to obey.

When the cords of guilt surround me
Then I will turn to keep Your ways.
Cords of guilt are loosed from round me
As I rise to sing Your praise.

Psalm
119:65-72   TET

Teach me judgment that is good
and deal fairly with me by Your word
for I have believed in Your commands,
learned by the afflictions of Your hand
the truth that my heart should keep.

The godless have hearts of fat,
and smear all the righteous with their lies
but that, Lord, is not Your servant's way,
who preserves Your precepts and delights
in Your law more than in wealth.

בְּחֻקֶּיךָ--
אֵבוֹשׁ.

Psalm **י** YUD
119:73-80

Your hands, O Lord, have made me,
    fashioned me firm.
Those who fear You see me
    rejoice in Thee
For they know how I tarry
    to wait Your word.

    Make me discern
    So I may learn
    All You command.

All the proud have bent me down
with their falsehood.
Your right judgments have bound me
in fidelity.
Let mercy, Lord, console me,
as You told me.

Make me discern
So I may learn
All You command.

בְחֻקֶּיךָ--
אֵבוֹשׁ.

Open compassion's womb
　　and hold me there
'Til I live to make Your law
　　my deep delight.
Help me to know Your precepts;
　　show me truth, Lord.

　　Make me discern
　　So I may learn
　　All You command.

Let those who fear You turn back
    and look at me
And see how my heart's complete
    and without shame.
Your hands, O Lord, have made me,
    fashioned me firm.

    Make me discern
    So I may learn
    All You command.

כ KAF

Keep me, Lord! Help me!

That which breathes within me is spent
in longing for Your deliverance;
I tarry for Your word.

My eyes are failing, consumed
for Your word, begging,
"when will You comfort me?"

Although I have become like a skin
in thick smoke, useless and shriveled,
I have not forgotten Your statutes.

How long shall Your servant live,
how many days until You bring judgment
on those who are chasing me?

From outside of Your way
the proud have dug traps to snare me,
like pits for catching lions.

I am chased after falsely, hunted,
so, hide me! Help me!
All Your commands are faithfulness.

As though it were nothing,
they almost consumed me in the land,
but I have not abandoned Your precepts.

Quicken me, O Lord;
according to Your lovingkindness,
I will keep the testimony of Your words.

Help me, Lord! Keep me!

Psalm
119:89-96  LAMED

Lord, Your word is firmly fixed in the heavens,
and Your faithfulness endures through generations.

You have established the earth so it stands fast;
all that You have made will serve You to the last.

I am Yours; save me.

Had Your whole law not been my constant delight,
then surely I would have perished in my plight.

Lord, I have refused to forget Your precepts;
when I made my dwelling in them, my life You kept.

I am Yours; save me.

When the wicked lie in wait to destroy me,
then I turn to ponder Your testimonies.

All else that seemed perfect has come to its end;
Your commandments without limit will extend.

I am Yours; save me.

אֶתְבּוֹנָן:
נָצָרְתִּי.

Psalm
119:97-104  MEM

My meditation is Your law
and I love to muse upon it
all the day long.

Your commandments make me wiser
than my enemies and keep me
all the day long.

I ponder Your testimonies
and they are sustenance for me
all the day long.

I guard Your precepts faithfully;
hold my feet back from the evil way
all the day long.

I walk the way that You direct.
Your word is honey in my mouth
all the day long.

Your law is my meditation
and I love to muse upon it
all the day long.

וָאֲקַיְּמָה
צְדָקֶךָ.

Psalm
119:105-112 נ NUN

Now, O Lord, make me alive
　　　　by Your quickening word,
for I have been sorely distressed
　　　　doing what I could
to keep from wandering
toward the snare the wicked set.

Your word is the only lamp
　　　　by which I guide my feet,
the light illumining my path
　　　　in the way most sweet
of Your righteous judgments
that I have sworn to fulfill.

Be pleased with me now, O Lord,
        as I offer freely
to place my soul into Your hand
        continually.
I will stretch out my heart
to possess Your testimonies.

ס SAMECH

Support me according to Your word
so that I may live.
And let me never be ashamed
so I may hope.

You toss aside those who stray
in treachery and falsehood.
Like dross You melt them away
and my flesh bristles from fear.

You are shield and hiding place
and I tarry for Your word.
But I despise all the halfhearted
who disdain what You command.

Sustain me in liberation
so that I may live.
Let me gaze in adoration
so I may hope.

כֹּל יִשַּׁרְתִּי
שֶׁקֶר

עַ AYIN

I am Your servant
and I have done
what is good and right,
so pledge to me, Lord,
the good that comes
from Your righteous word.

My eyes are consumed,
only fulfilled,
by Your salvation
and declaration
of Your commands
I love more than gold.

It is time to act
for me, O Lord;
do not forsake me
to my oppressors
or let the proud
harm or distress me.

Deal with Your servant
who has followed
Your testimonies
and hated falsehood
so faithfully;
give lovingkindness.

Lord, I want to know
all Your statutes;
give understanding
that I may follow
the smooth pathway.
I am Your servant.

Psalm
119:129-136   פ PEY

Pull from Your pouch of justice
the lot of grace for me,
mercy as right judgment
for my iniquity.

Let Your unfolding words,
as sun and moon, give light
to make the simple wise,
to keep Your precepts right.

Let Your holy face shine
on Your servant this day;
establish every footfall
to keep me in Your way.

Rescued from oppression,
the hold of evil men;
teach me by Your statutes,
deliver me from sin.

Show me Your testimonies,
Your wonders to impart;
I pant for Your commands,
the longings of my heart.

My eyes run like channels
for all the things I saw,
for the ransomed people
who failed to keep Your law.

Pull from Your pouch of justice
the lot of grace for me,
mercy as right judgment
for my iniquity.

הֲבִינֵנִי וְאֶחְיֶה.

צ TSADE

Zeal, like the ardor of a jealous husband,
overwhelms me because my adversaries
have all forgotten Your word.

But You are the eternal righteous one, Lord,
and Your testimonies are straight and steadfast
and Your judgments all are good.

I am so despised and insignificant
and yet I have never forgotten Your law,
precepts that are ever true.

When my enemies and distress have found me
then Your commandments are my intense delight;
Your servant so loves Your word!

Your righteousness is righteousness eternal.
Make me discern Your endless testimonies
for they will give me new life.

וָאֲשַׁוְּעָה;
יִחָלְתִּי.

Psalm
119:145-152 QOPH

Quicken me, O Lord,
according to Your lovingkindness;
listen to me, Lord,
for I am pursued by wickedness.

They have turned away
and have become distant from Your law;
my eyes meet the watches,
ponder Your promises night and dawn.

My whole heart cries out,
answer me so I keep Your statutes;
liberate me, Lord,
that I may guard Your testimonies.

From the bright east, Lord,
as from the beginning, I have known
that You are near me—
Your commands are faithfulness alone.

וָאֶתְקוֹטְטָה-
לֹא שָׁמָרוּ.

ר RAYSH

Rescue me, Lord,
from my afflictions
that I have suffered
when I forget Your holy law.

Redeem me, Lord,
and be my kinsman;
take up my struggle,
and by Your word make me alive.

Long have I looked on the deceitful
and loathed those who discount Your word.

Many are my persecutors
yet from Your way I am not moved.

See how I have loved Your precepts
and Your right judgments evermore.

Rescue me, Lord,
from my afflictions
that I have suffered
when I forget Your holy law.

Redeem me, Lord,
and be my kinsman;
take up my struggle,
and by Your word make me alive.

 _Psalm_
119:161-168
SHIN

Seven times each day I sing praise,

I exult at Your righteous sayings.

My soul keeps Your precepts all my days

so that my journey is by Your leading—

I turn from falsehoods I abhor

and wait for Your salvation, Lord.

The powerful chase me without any cause,
and yet my heart stands in awe of Your words,
finds peace abundant in Your Torah[2]
that makes my steps so I do not stumble—
I turn from falsehoods I abhor
and wait for Your salvation, Lord.

---

[2] The proper noun *Torah* most commonly refers to the Pentateuch or Five Books of
Moses. Here and in the Tav section that follows, Torah is the same Hebrew word that
is rendered as "law," "holy law," or "law of God" elsewhere in this volume.

  TAV

Torah is my intense delight.
Let my soul live and let it praise You.

Torah is my intense delight.
Allow my ringing cry before Your face.

Torah is my intense delight.
Keep Your wandering sheep from perishing.

Torah is my intense delight.
Deliver me, Lord, by Your just saying.

Torah is my intense delight.
My tongue and my lips will spring forth with song.

Torah is my intense delight.
Let Your hand be my help and salvation.

Torah is my intense delight.
Teach me by Your statutes and commandments.

Torah is my intense delight.
Seek me, Your servant, Lord, as Your own flock.

Torah is my intense delight.
Let my soul live and let it praise You.

Bibliography

Brown, Francis, S. Driver, and C. Briggs. *Brown-Driver-Briggs Hebrew and English Lexicon*. Peabody, MA: Hendrickson Publishers, 1996.

Elliger, Karl, and Willhelm Rudolph, editors. *Biblia Hebraica Stuttgartensia (Hebrew Edition)*. Peabody, MA: Hendrikson Publishers, 2006.

The Holy Bible: English Standard Version. Wheaton, IL: Crossway Bibles, 2001.

The Hymnal 1982: According to the Use of the Episcopal Church. New York: Church Publishing Inc., 1985.

Lewis, C.S. *Reflections on the Psalms*. New York: Harvest Books, 1986.

Tanakh: A New Translation of the Holy Scriptures According to the Traditional Hebrew Text. Philadelphia: The Jewish Publication Society, 1985.

Further Reading

The Book of Psalms: A New Translation According to the Traditional Hebrew Text. Philadelphia: The Jewish Publication Society, 1997.

Davie, Donald, editor. *The Psalms in English*. New York: Penguin Books, 1996.

Tickle, Phyllis, compiler. *The Divine Hours Pocket Edition*. New York: Oxford University Press, 2007.

About Paraclete Press

Who We Are

Paraclete Press is a publisher of books, recordings, and DVDs on Christian spirituality. Our publishing represents a full expression of Christian belief and practice—from Catholic to Evangelical, from Protestant to Orthodox.

We are the publishing arm of the Community of Jesus, an ecumenical monastic community in the Benedictine tradition. As such, we are uniquely positioned in the marketplace without connection to a large corporation and with informal relationships to many branches and denominations of faith.

What We Are Doing

Books

Paraclete publishes books that show the richness and depth of what it means to be Christian. Although Benedictine spirituality is at the heart of all that we do, we publish books that reflect the Christian experience across many cultures, time periods, and houses of worship. We publish books that nourish the vibrant life of the church and its people—books about spiritual practice, formation, history, ideas, and customs.

We have several different series, including the best-selling Living Library, Paraclete Essentials, and Paraclete Giants series of classic texts in contemporary English; A Voice from the Monastery—men and women monastics writing about living a spiritual life today; award-winning literary faith fiction and poetry; and the Active Prayer Series that brings creativity and liveliness to any life of prayer.

Recordings

From Gregorian chant to contemporary American choral works, our music recordings celebrate sacred choral music through the centuries. Paraclete distributes the recordings of the internationally acclaimed choir Gloriæ Dei Cantores, praised for their "rapt and fathomless spiritual intensity" by *American Record Guide*, and the Gloriæ Dei Cantores Schola, which specializes in the study and performance of Gregorian chant. Paraclete is also the exclusive North American distributor of the recordings of the Monastic Choir of St. Peter's Abbey in Solesmes, France, long considered to be a leading authority on Gregorian chant.

DVDs

Our DVDs offer spiritual help, healing, and biblical guidance for life issues: grief and loss, marriage, forgiveness, anger management, facing death, and spiritual formation.

Learn more about us at our Web site:
www.paracletepress.com, or call us toll-free at 1-800-451-5006.

You may also be interested in . . .

The Paraclete Psalter
A Book of Daily Prayer

ISBN: 978-1-55725-663-8
$18.99, Flex-hardcover

It was common practice among the early Christians to pray the entire book of Psalms each month. Now, you can enter into this rewarding practice with this beautifully designed, easy-to-follow prayer book. Featuring the NIV text, *The Paraclete Psalter* will guide you through the entire psalmody every four weeks.

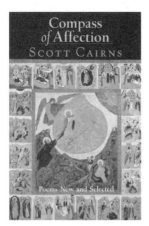

The Compass of Affection
Poems New and Selected
by Scott Cairns

ISBN: 978-1-55725-503-7
$25, Hardcover

Scott Cairns expresses an immediate, incarnate theology of God's power and presence in the world. Spanning thirty years and including selections from four of his previous collections, *Compass of Affection* presents the best of his work—the holy made tangible, love made flesh, and theology performed rather than discussed.

Available from Paraclete Press
www.paracletepress.com • 1-800-451-5006